PARTICIPANT'S GUIDE   8 SESSIONS

WOUNDED

IN THE

CHURCH

RAY BEESON & CHRIS HAYWARD

WOUNDED IN THE CHURCH

WHITAKER
HOUSE

Wounded in the Church Participant's Guide

ISBN: 978-1-62911-934-2
Printed in the United States of America
© 2017 by Ray Beeson and Chris Hayward

Whitaker House
1030 Hunt Valley Circle
New Kensington, PA 15068
www.whitakerhouse.com

1 2 3 4 5 6 7 8 9 10 11 ⊔⊔ 24 23 22 21 20 19 18 17

CONTENTS

HOW TO USE THIS GUIDE

You might be thinking, *A participant's guide? How can I possibly talk about the pain that I've experienced in church—it's too personal!* Or, on the other hand, your reaction might be, *Finally! A chance to express what's frustrated me for years about my church!* Wherever you land on the spectrum of Christians who have experienced the wounding that happens in church, we truly believe that you will benefit from taking the material in *Wounded in the Church* and personally applying it through these pages.

The *Guide* is designed to aid and inspire group discussion about a touchy topic. Although some of the discussion questions may seem too probing, we leave it up to your discretion to answer only those you feel comfortable addressing.

There are eight sessions in the guide, making it an easy 8-week fit for a church group such as a Bible study or Sunday school class. To aid discussion leaders, an all-original DVD is also available in which we introduce each session's topic.

We also wanted a *Guide* that could be used for individual devotion and reflection. The material in the book is heavy stuff, and we know some readers will need room to reflect, journal, and pray through the topics that are presented. Those were the readers we had in mind when we wrote the "Personal Reflection" questions.

Under "Read," we included Scriptures that we felt were pertinent to the topic. We hope you'll never just take our word for it, but rather again and again dive back into the Bible to discern whether what we are saying is true. And in each session under "Ponder," we compiled quotations that sparked our interest, culled from a variety of sources. Since our own perspective is limited even as we write on these issues, what better way to widen the perspective than by expanding the conversation? May the thoughtfulness of the authors' quotations provoke insights of your own.

Finally, each session closes with a prayer or a suggestion for prayer. Nothing so binds us to our Father as does earnest, fervent prayer—especially in the face of revived pain, remembered hurt, or a revelation of what we need to do. Whether alone or in a group, and whether using our suggestion or not, never fail to *"seek the* LORD*"* (Isaiah 55:6).

We pray that God will use this guide to promote participation, discussion, reflection, prayer, and worship that heals wounded hearts in the way that only God can.

In that hope,
Ray Beeson and Chris Hayward

INTRODUCTION
EXPECTATIONS OF CHURCH

Read Chapter One:
I Thought Church Would Be Different

OPENING DISCUSSION:

1. Which of these statements do you identify with most? Why?

[ ] Christianity is about being as good as we can possibly be.

[ ] Christianity and all other religions lead to the same place.

[ ] Christianity is about developing a personal relationship with God.

[ ] Christianity has done more bad for the world than it has done good.

2. How many people can you think of who eventually left the church because of some offense?

3. Are Christians better than other people?

PONDER:

> The gospel is this: We are more sinful and flawed in ourselves than we ever dared believe, yet at the very same time we are more loved and accepted in Jesus Christ than we ever dared hope. —*Timothy J. Keller*[1]

> The contemporary Church is so often a weak, ineffectual voice with an uncertain sound. It is so often the arch supporter of the status quo. Far from being disturbed by the presence of the Church, the power structure of the average community is consoled by the Church's silent and often vocal sanction of things as they are.
>
> —*Dr. Martin Luther King, Jr.*[2]

---

1. Tim Keller, *The Meaning of Marriage* (New York: Penguin, 2013),
2. Martin Luther King, Jr, "Letter from a Birmingham Jail," April 16, 1963.

SESSION ONE
THE PAIN

SESSION ONE

THE PAIN

Read Chapters 2–3:
The Pain Goes So Deep
Where Does All This Pain Come From?

DISCUSSION QUESTIONS:

1. Out of every one hundred people, how many do you think are hurting on a regular basis? Out of every one hundred Christians, how many do you think are hurting? Why?

2. How would you answer someone who denies that emotional pain is a big deal?

3. Can you think of some ways that God stretched you by leaving some deep pain in your life for longer than you expected?

4. Do you sometimes feel that life is tough for you personally because of the wrong things you've done in the past? Do you feel that God is still punishing you for your sins?

5. Have you ever felt that no matter what you try to do to please God, it doesn't seem to work?

6. How do you think the church today is different from the church in the time of New Testament?

7. Do you find comfort in meeting in groups, or is that one of your sources of fear?

8. Describe the worst thing you've ever gone through as a result of an experience with a church. Does it fit into any of the sources of pain listed in chapter 3 (thinking that never tries to auto-correct; inability to listen; inability to disagree; isolationism; a religious spirit; suspicion; favoritism)?

9. What other sources of emotional pain inflicted by the church would you add to the list in chapter 3?

10. What does isolationism look like in the twenty-first century? Where have you seen cases of spiritual isolationism?

FOR PERSONAL REFLECTION:

1. If you have felt emotional pain in the past, do you consider yourself recovered from it? Or are you still in the middle of dealing with it?

2. Who are some people you can look to for help and guidance if you are in the middle of dealing with emotional pain, or in case you were to experience it in the future? What steps can you take to personally find such people?

3. Often people become controlling because they fear being controlled by others. Have you noticed this negative type of control in your own life? Have you ever felt that when someone could not control you, they subsequently rejected you? On the flip side, consider whether you have rejected others because you could not control them.

READ:

Blessed be the God and Father of our Lord Jesus Christ, the Father of mercies and God of all comfort, who comforts us in all our tribulation, that we may be able to comfort those who are in any trouble, with the comfort with which we ourselves are comforted by God. For as the sufferings of Christ abound in us, so our consolation also abounds through Christ. Now if we are afflicted, it is for your consolation and salvation, which is effective for enduring the same sufferings which we also suffer. Or if we are comforted, it is for your consolation and salvation. And our hope for you is steadfast, because we know that as you are partakers of the sufferings, so also you will partake of the consolation.

(2 Corinthians 1:3-7)

For we do not have a High Priest who cannot sympathize with our weaknesses, but was in all points tempted as we are, yet without sin. Let us therefore come boldly to the throne of grace, that we may obtain mercy and find grace to help in time of need.

(Hebrews 4:15-16)

PONDER:

"I would have become a Christian if it were not for Christians." —attributed to Mahatma Gandhi

"From the beginning, the followers of Jesus Christ knew they were not just members of an organization, nor did they think they were an extension of Old Testament Judaism. They knew they were followers of the living Lord Jesus Christ. They had seen His resurrected body, had touched Him, eaten with Him, and talked to Him. They knew they were members of a new thing—the church—His body, and that the church could transform the world." —Elmer L. Towns[3]

"Jesus Christ lived in the midst of his enemies. At the end all his disciples deserted him. On the Cross he was utterly alone, surrounded by evildoers and mockers. For this cause he had come, to bring peace to the enemies of God. So the Christian, too, belongs not in the seclusion of a cloistered life but in the thick of foes. There is his commission, his work. 'The kingdom is to be in the midst of your enemies. And he who will not suffer this does not want to be of the Kingdom of Christ; he wants to be among friends, to sit among roses and lilies, not with the bad people but the devout people. O you blasphemers and betrayers of Christ! If Christ had done what you are doing, who would ever have been spared?' (Luther)." —Dietrich Bonhoeffer[4]

---

3. Elmer L. Towns, *What's Right with the Church* (Ventura, CA: Regal, 2009), 7.
4. Dietrich Bonhoeffer, *Life Together* (New York: Harper and Row, 1954), 17–18.

AS YOU PRAY:

Remember that God knows your heart and the pain you carry. His request is that you talk to Him about it. His desire is that you put everything else aside; your guilt, your anger, and whatever it is that fills your mind right now. All of us pray a little differently, but the subject of pain is still the same. With reverence, let Him know your heart and your heartaches.

> *Father God, if You will listen to me, I want to talk to you about things that have been hurting me for a long time—including the church. You know how I've been treated and how I feel about them. I don't want to be this way. I want to love You and Your people. But I'm confused about how to deal with them.*

[In your own words, specifically tell Him the things that have hurt you deeply. Your prayer might be different from the above, simply let it flow from your heart.]

SESSION TWO

NEGLECT
AND REJECTION

SESSION TWO
NEGLECT AND REJECTION

Read Chapters 4–5:
Nobody Sees Me
I Feel Beat Up in Church

DISCUSSION QUESTIONS:

1. On a scale of 1 to 10, how often do you feel neglected by the church? _____. If you put a number higher than "1," describe one such instance.

2. On a scale of 1 to 10, how often do you feel rejected by the church? _____. If you put a number higher than "1," describe one such instance.

3. Why is neglect so hurtful?

4. What does the story of Hagar in Genesis 16 tell us about neglect?

5. How would you answer somebody in a church context who earnestly desires to accept, not neglect, but doesn't know how?

6. What are the two kinds of rejection, and where have you seen them in your own life?

7. What do you think the answer is to Rodney King's question, "Why can't we all just get along?" in context of churches and Christian denominations? Explain.

8. Have you ever felt, in a church situation, that you had to behave in a particular manner to please the people around you? How did you feel about those rules; were they helpful or unhelpful in your Christian walk?

9. Have you ever been spiritually abused? Explain if you are able to freely and comfortably do so.

10. What's a healthy way to leave a healthy church? What's a healthy way to leave an unhealthy church? Have you ever been in that position?

FOR PERSONAL REFLECTION:

1. If you could serve in a church, in what capacity would you like to do so? Is there anything hindering you from serving in that capacity?

2. Take a look at your life and the people who have rejected you. Write down their names. As you read through *Wounded in the Church*, keep that list handy and ask yourself over a period of days or weeks, *Does it still hurt when I think of them? Have I forgiven them? How can I forgive them?* (See chapter 8.)

3. Have you ever blamed yourself for rejection you have experienced? Have you ever blamed God?

READ:

*Then those of you who escape will remember Me among the nations where they are carried captive, because **I was crushed** by their adulterous heart which has departed from Me, and by their eyes which play the harlot after their idols; they will loathe themselves for the evils which they committed in all their abominations.* (Ezekiel 6:9)

But first He must suffer many things and be rejected by this generation. (Luke 17:25)

But God composed the body, having given greater honor to that part which lacks it, that there should be no schism in the body, but that the members should have the same care for one another. And if one member suffers, all the members suffer with it; or if one member is honored, all the members rejoice with it. (1 Corinthians 12:24-26)

PONDER:

"I've learned that people will forget what you said, people will forget what you did, but people will never forget how you made them feel."　　　　　　　　　　—Carl Buehner

"Do you know what hurts so very much? It's love. Love is the strongest force in the world, and when it is blocked that means pain. There are two things we can do when this happens. We can kill that love so that it stops hurting. But then of course part of us dies, too. Or we can ask God to open up another route for that love to travel."　　　—Corrie ten Boom[5]

"He that cleaveth unto creatures [people], shall fall with that which is frail; he that embraceth Jesus, shall stand firmly for ever. Love Him and keep Him for thy friend, who, when all go away, will not forsaking thee, nor suffer thee to perish in the end."　　　　　　　　　　　—Thomas á Kempis[6]

"Being unwanted, unloved, uncared for, forgotten by everybody, I think that is a much greater poverty than the person who has nothing to eat."　　　　　　　—Mother Teresa

---

5. Corrie Ten Boom with John and Elizabeth Sherrill, *The Hiding Place* (Washington Depot, CT: Chosen, 1971), 47.
6. Thomas á Kempis, *Imitation of Christ* (Chicago: Moody, 1980), 102–103.

AS YOU PRAY:

Father God, the things that I have been going through have left me hopeless. I just need to know that someone cares. As I am learning more about You, I have found that what I'm going through, You have also gone through. Can You help me?

Remember that in the days ahead, He will speak to you. He will do so in ways that may amaze you; through His written word, through people who know Him well, and through a still small voice directly into your heart. Wait for Him to speak in ways that you know it is His voice.

[Your prayer might be different from the above, simply let it flow from your heart.]

SESSION THREE

SHAME,
MANIPULATION,
LONELINESS

SHAME, MANIPULATION, LONELINESS

Read Chapters 6–7:
I Live in Shame All the Time
I Feel Used

DISCUSSION QUESTIONS:

1. What's the difference between guilt and shame?

2. Do you recall a time when you were made to feel ashamed in church? If so, share the experience.

3. What was the lie you believed because of that shame? Were you able to deal with that shame, or are you still reeling from the pain?

4. Which promise on page 84 resonated the most with you? Why?

5. In what way has the pain you experienced in church life affected you? In what way has life's pain in general affected you?

6. What impact has grace made on your life?

7. Has wrong teaching ever been a source of pain for you? When you dis-covered the truth to contradict that wrong teaching, how did it help in the healing process?

8. Have you ever asked the question, *Why is the world so mean and intolerant?* How do you think God sees the world with all of its trouble?

9. Try to define a controlling attitude in your own words. List some of your run-ins with this attitude. Did you win or lose? Share if you can.

10. Do you think it's possible for a church to hurt its leader, or is it only those in authority who have the power to wound?

FOR PERSONAL REFLECTION:

1. Have you ever been told by a church that you were beyond the reach of, or too sinful for, God? Have you ever felt that you did something too terrible for God to forgive?

2. Think about the shame you have experienced. Is it helpful to identify that shame as a certain type, as listed in chapter 6?

3. In what ways have the pride and arrogance of leaders in your life (family, workplace, church, community, government) caused you pain?

READ:

For the Lord God will help Me;
Therefore I will not be disgraced;
Therefore I have set My face like a flint,
And I know that I will not be ashamed.　　　　　(Isaiah 50:7)

No temptation has overtaken you except such as is common to man; but God is faithful, who will not allow you to be tempted beyond what you are able, but with the temptation will also make the way of escape, that you may be able to bear it.

(1 Corinthians 10:13)

Now may the God of peace Himself sanctify you completely; and may your whole spirit, soul, and body be preserved blameless at the coming of our Lord Jesus Christ. He who calls you is faithful, who also will do it.　　　　　(1 Thessalonians 5:23–24)

PONDER:

"When you are in the midst of testing, do not give up in despair. Faith is a dogged grace! Unless your soul flatly denies the power of God, this courier—faith—will beat a well-worn path to the throne. Doubt cripples but does not incapacitate faith. Indeed, even as you are disputing the mercy of God and questioning in your mind whether He will come to your rescue, faith will make its way, if haltingly, into His presence."   —William Gurnall[7]

"Don't you think the things people are most ashamed of are things they can't help?"   —C.S. Lewis[8]

"Are you a believer and afraid of your old sins? You are afraid of foes which do not exist. Your sins are so gone that they cannot be laid to your charge…. You are not only pardoned, but you are a child of God. Go to your Father with joy and thankfulness, and bless him for all his love to you. Wipe those tears away, smooth those wrinkles from your brow: take up the song of joy and gladness."   —Charles Spurgeon[9]

---

7. William Gurnall, *The Christian in Complete Armour*, vol. 1 (Carlisle, PA: The Banner Of Truth Trust, 1986), 45.

8. C. S. Lewis, *Till We Have Faces*, (San Diego: Harcourt, 1980), 111.

9. Charles Spurgeon, "Plenary Absolution" (Sermon 1108, MTP 19:239), http://center. spurgeon.org/2016/09/13/13-spurgeon-quotes-for-fighting-sin-and-shame/.

AS YOU PRAY:

Remember that as embarrassing as some events are, God is not surprised by anything. There is nothing you have done or has been done to you that He is not interested in talking to you about. Learning what His love means has the power to shatter every evil thing that has ever touched your life.

Father God, I feel so undone. There's a huge void inside of me. My guilt and shame overwhelms me at times. I so much want to get rid of it.

[Your prayer might be different, simply let it flow from your heart.]

FORGIVENESS AND MOVING PAST PAIN

FORGIVENESS AND MOVING PAST PAIN

Read Chapters 8–9:
I Can't Forgive
Will I Ever Get Past the Pain?

DISCUSSION QUESTIONS:

1. Have you ever had trouble forgiving someone? Has the matter been taken care of or does it still persist?

2. If you still have trouble forgiving someone, can you think of ways it may be affecting your life?

3. What kinds of thoughts refresh old pain? What happens when you try to stop those thoughts?

4. Have you ever asked for forgiveness, received it, and then felt disappointed because the other person didn't ask for forgiveness, too? Why do you think that happens?

5. Has anyone refused to forgive you as a method of controlling you? How did you respond? Did you get past that control tactic?

6. Do you believe it is possible to forgive someone who has not repented? Why?

7. Do you think it's possible that thoughts which produce pain are sometimes satanically induced?

8. Do you ever feel like something is making your mind think about bad things even though you don't want to?

9. Is it hard for you to set boundaries in your relationships? If able, explain.

10. Was there a time when you felt needed in the church? Too needed? Not needed enough? Explain.

FOR PERSONAL REFLECTION:

1. Even after you have forgiven someone, negative thoughts about the situation will probably still enter your mind. Does that nullify your forgiveness? Explain.

2. Is there someone whom you need to forgive, but cannot get in touch with? Some reasons might be concerns for safety, a long distance, a nonexistent relationship because it happened long in the past or happened without the knowledge of the offender, or the death of the offender. Remember that even if you can't forgive personally, you can then turn to God and share with Him your situation and your willingness to forgive.

3. Is it possible to be offended by God? Is it ever appropriate to forgive Him?

READ:

Take heed to yourselves. If your brother sins against you, rebuke him; and if he repents, forgive him. And if he sins against you seven times in a day, and seven times in a day returns to you, saying, "I repent," you shall forgive him. (Luke 17:3–4)

And not only that, but we also glory in tribulations, knowing that tribulation produces perseverance; and perseverance, character; and character, hope. (Romans 5:3–4)

And God will wipe away every tear from their eyes; there shall be no more death, nor sorrow, nor crying. There shall be no more pain, for the former things have passed away. (Revelation 21:4)

PONDER:

"The glory of Christianity is to conquer by forgiveness."

—William Blake

"We never know how God will answer our prayers, but we can expect that He will get us involved in His plan for the answer. If we are true intercessors, we must be ready to take part in God's work on behalf of the people for whom we pray."

—Corrie ten Boom[10]

"Without a friend thou canst not well live; and if Jesus be not above all a friend to thee, thou shalt be indeed sad and desolate."

—Thomas á Kempis[11]

"The difference between shallow happiness and a deep, sustaining joy is sorrow. Happiness lives where sorrow is not. When sorrow arrives, happiness dies. It can't stand pain. Joy, on the other hand, rises from sorrow and therefore can withstand all grief. Joy, by the grace of God, is the transfiguration of suffering into endurance, and of endurance into character, and of character into hope—and the hope that has become our joy does not (as happiness must for those who depend upon it) disappoint us."

—Walter Wangerin Jr.[12]

10. Cited in Pam Rosewell Moore, *Life Lessons from the Hiding Place* (Grand Rapids, MI: Chosen, 2004), 38.
11. Kempis, *Imitation of Christ*, 105.
12. Walter Wangerin, Jr., *Reliving the Passion* (Grand Rapids, MI: Zondervan, 1992), 31.

AS YOU PRAY:

Remember that God has promised that if you will come to him, He will accept you with all of your problems, including unforgiveness. It's here He can show you a very valuable thing: when you ask for His help, He will give to you through the indwelling Holy Spirit. For it is God who works in you both to *want* to do good and then to *do* it.

> *Father God, I hate a lot of people for what they've done to me. I also know it's tearing me to pieces, but I just can't forgive them. They've caused too much pain. I've heard that if I don't forgive them, you will not forgive me for the wrong things I've done. That scares me. But how do I get rid of these seething feelings? Father God, if you want to work in me to help me to do what I can't do and most of the time don't want to do, I'm a candidate for your help.*

[Your prayer might be different, simply let it flow from your heart.]

IDENTITY AND THE
ROLE OF THE LAW

SESSION FIVE
IDENTITY AND THE ROLE OF THE LAW

Read Chapters 10–11:
Why Do I Feel So Unsafe in Church?
I Can't Keep Up with All the Rules

DISCUSSION QUESTIONS:

1. Have you ever asked God what your identity is? What did He say?

2. What do you think it means to be *"in Christ"*? (See, for example, Romans 6:23.)

3. Do you believe that Jesus wants to destroy the "bad" of your past and give you a new identity? What would you like your new identity to look like?

4. What makes you feel safe in church? How can you make others feel safe in church?

5. Do you feel that rules help or hinder you in your Christian walk?

6. Have you ever been in a church where they had a fairly extensive set of "rules"? How did you respond to them?

7. Have you ever been wounded in a church by violating a church rule? How did that wound come? Who inflicted it? How has this pain affected other areas of your life?

8. How did Jesus deal with rule-breakers? Can you give some examples from the Gospels?

9. What is the role of "rules" or "the Law" in the Christian church?

10. Is it okay to ignore a church's rule if it is extrabiblical (not found in the Bible)? Is it ok to *obey* an extrabiblical rule?

FOR PERSONAL REFLECTION:

1. Have you ever considered the possibility of a deeply caring attitude being at the top of all of God's commandments? How would that change your life?

2. Do you believe that God wants to help you in the midst of your struggles no matter how you got there? Or, do you find yourself believing that God won't listen to you until you get your life cleaned up?

3. Do you view your spiritual life more as a big "To Do" list or as a relationship?

READ:

"Before I formed you in the womb I knew you;
Before you were born I sanctified you....
Do not be afraid of their faces,
For I am with you to deliver you," says the LORD.

(Jeremiah 1:5, 8)

Therefore, my brethren, you also have become dead to the law through the body of Christ, that you may be married to another—to Him who was raised from the dead, that we should bear fruit to God. For when we were in the flesh, the sinful passions which were aroused by the law were at work in our members to bear fruit to death. But now we have been delivered from the law, having died to what we were held by, so that we should serve in the newness of the Spirit and not in the oldness of the letter

(Romans 7:4-6)

To them God willed to make known what are the riches of the glory of this mystery among the Gentiles: which is Christ in you, the hope of glory.

(Colossians 1:27)

PONDER:

"The law tells me how crooked I am. Grace comes along and straightens me out."   —Dwight L. Moody

"Nothing humbles and breaks the heart of a sinner like mercy and love. Souls that converse much with sin and wrath, may be much terrified; but souls the converse much with grace and mercy, will be much humbled."   —Thomas Brooks[13]

"The reason why many are still troubled, still seeking, still making little forward progress is because they haven't yet come to the end of themselves. We're still trying to give orders, and interfering with God's work within us."

—A. W. Tozer

"Christianity preaches the infinite worth of that which is seemingly worthless and the infinite worthlessness of that which is seemingly so valued."   —Dietrich Bonhoeffer[14]

---

13. Thomas Brooks, *The Select Works of Thomas Brooks*, vol. 1 (London: L. B. Seeley and Son, 1824), 39.
14. Dietrich Bonhoeffer, "Jesus Christ and the Essence of Christianity," *The Bonhoeffer Reader* (Minneapolis, MN: Fortress Press, 2013), 355.

PRAYER:

Father God, I get so confused about the do's and dont's of life. The confusion makes me not want to go to church or even hang out with Christians. Why is just doing Your will so complicated? People tell me You're a loving God, but I have no experiences to prove that. It seems that every time I turn around somebody tells me I'm wrong about what I'm doing. I usually know when something is really wrong and often I really don't want to do it. But it's this constant, "is this right or is it wrong?" I need your help. I don't want to be this way and something deep inside tells me that you're not a God of doubt.

[Your prayer might be different from the above, simply let it flow from your heart.]

THE RELIGIOUS SPIRIT AND PERFECTIONISM

THE RELIGIOUS SPIRIT AND PERFECTIONISM

Read Chapters 12–13:
What Wrong with These People?
I Just Need to Be Perfect

DISCUSSION QUESTIONS:

1. Do you believe demons can attack Christians? Why or why not? If yes, how do they do so?

2. Do you believe that good people can sometimes be deceived? Can you think of any?

3. Have you ever been deceived and had to admit it?

4. What tactics of the enemy have you seen in your own life?

5. What is your definition of the "religious spirit"?

6. Have you ever found out that something you once believed in wasn't really true? What did you do? How did it affect you?

7. Have you ever had a friend believe in something about which you had a doubt, but which later proved to be true despite your doubt? How did you respond?

8. Can you see ways in which the enemy of your soul led you to believe something that was in error?

9. Do you think perfectionism is a form of arrogance? Explain.

10. Have you ever experienced the way perfectionism can drive a person into fear and anxiety? Explain.

FOR PERSONAL REFLECTION:

1. Have you ever been hurt by a religious activist? Any kind of activist? Is "extremism" always a bad thing?

2. If you are a perfectionist, how would you describe your perfectionism?

3. What's the opposite of perfectionism? Do you struggle with it?

READ:

Therefore I hated life because the work that was done under the sun was distressing to me, for all is vanity and grasping for the wind. Then I hated all my labor in which I had toiled under the sun, because I must leave it to the man who will come after me. And who knows whether he will be wise or a fool? Yet he will rule over all my labor in which I toiled and in which I have shown myself wise under the sun. This also is vanity. (Ecclesiastes 2:17-19)

For there is no difference; for all have sinned and fall short of the glory of God, being justified freely by His grace through the redemption that is in Christ Jesus. (Romans 3:22-24)

Beloved, do not believe every spirit, but test the spirits, whether they are of God; because many false prophets have gone out into the world. By this you know the Spirit of God: Every spirit that confesses that Jesus Christ has come in the flesh is of God, and every spirit that does not confess that Jesus Christ has come in the flesh is not of God. And this is the spirit of the Antichrist, which you have heard was coming, and is now already in the world. (1 John 4:1-3)

PONDER:

"You can safely assume you've created God in your own image when it turns out that God hates all the same people you do."   —Anne Lamott[15]

"Today there is a strong emphasis in certain religious circles which insists that the ideal spiritual life is one of unbroken joy, peace, and material prosperity. The impression is current that to be saved and filled with the Spirit opens a charmed life entirely trouble-free, where all problems are instantaneously solved and where miracles never cease. According to some, 'a miracle a day' is the norm. If one does not experience constant supernatural manifestations it is because he is subnormal spiritually. Something is wrong between him and God.... Certainly it is true that few of us live up to our spiritual privilege. God would love to manifest His generosity and miracle-working power far more than it is normally seen. But is this philosophy in proper spiritual perspective and balance or does it represent only one side of the coin?"   —Paul Billheimer[16]

"If you feel that you can follow a few little rules or some clever gimmicks to make you a mature Christian, then you have fallen into a subtle trap of legalism."   —J. Vernon McGee[17]

15. Anne Lamott, *Bird by Bird* (New York: Anchor, 1995), 22.
16. Paul Billheimer, *Don't Waste Your Sorrows* (Christian Literature Crusade, Fort Washington, PA, 1977), 18.
17. J. Vernon McGee, *1 and 2 Timothy / Titus / Philemon* (Nashville, TN: Thomas Nelson, 1991), chapter 2.

PRAYER:

Father God, I've met religious people who make my skin crawl. That's why I've never wanted anything to do with You. But now I'm finding those whom I think are genuine Christians. I like them and I'd like to be "like" them. If there's anything You can do to help me, please do. I'm open to the life I see in the people who serve You.

[Your prayer might be different from the above, simply let it flow from your heart.]

REJECTING CLICHÉS AND FINDING A CHURCH HOME

REJECTING CLICHÉS AND FINDING A CHURCH HOME

Read Chapters 14–15:
The Church Doesn't Seem to Care
How Do I Find a Good Church?

DISCUSSION QUESTIONS:

1. What do you think of people in general? Do you think they usually fail you or support you? Why?

2. What character attributes are you looking for in the people you go to church with?

3. Which clichés and statements in chapter 14 have you heard or said?

4. What does "Christian care" look like to you?

5. What do you think the solution is to mental and emotional pain?

6. Which "red flags" in church have you witnessed?

_____

_____

_____

_____

_____

_____

_____

_____

7. Do you believe there are good churches? Why or why not?

_____

_____

_____

_____

_____

_____

_____

_____

8. Were you ever in the position of looking for a new church home? What was that experience like?

9. What are some of the differences between good, powerful leadership and leadership that is corrupt and controlling? Who are the leaders that you respect?

10. Do you think God loves all people? Why or why not?

FOR PERSONAL REFLECTION:

1. Do you think God loves you? Why or why not?

2. Are you willing to trust again?

3. Which doctrines are "essential theology" to you? Make a list.

READ:

And let us consider one another in order to stir up love and good works, not forsaking the assembling of ourselves together, as is the manner of some, but exhorting one another, and so much the more as you see the Day approaching.   (Hebrews 10:24–25)

That which we have seen and heard we declare to you, that you also may have fellowship with us; and truly our fellowship is with the Father and with His Son Jesus Christ. And these things we write to you that your joy may be full.   (1 John 1:3–4)

PONDER:

"I want neither a terrorist spirituality that keeps me in a perpetual state of fright about being in right relationship with my heavenly Father nor a sappy spirituality that portrays God as such a benign teddy bear that there is no aberrant behavior or desire of mine that he will not condone. I want a relationship with the Abba of Jesus, who is infinitely compassionate with my brokenness and at the same time an awesome, incomprehensible, and unwieldy Mystery."   —Brennan Manning[18]

"Learning to trust is one of life's most difficult tasks."

—Isaac Watts

"I was faced with the problem. If morals, values, and relationships are the areas my clients struggle with the most, and difficulties in any one area can cause them to relapse, then what program can I send them to that has the teaching, support, and accountability in all of these areas? There is only one that I know of—the church. I began to ask myself, 'Whose problem is this?' I realized that if those of us in the helping ministries want our clients to be successful long-term, then it's up to me, and all Christians with a heart for wounded people, to create safe and effective churches."

—Michael Dye[19]

18. Brennan Manning, *Ruthless Trust* (New York: HarperCollins, 2009), 107.
19. Michael Dye, *The Church: Helping or Hurting?* (Auburn, CA: Genesis Publishing, 2015), 29–30.

AS YOU PRAY:

Remember that God wants His people to gather together for a number of reasons, including the safety in numbers and the comfort that comes from other like-minded people. But Christians who meet together have come under some of the most hideous demonic attacks anyone can fathom. At the same time they have found that the Holy Spirit works in us to keep us from falling. But it is a war. That's why the Scriptures speak so much about being armed in order to fight a very good fight.

> *Father God, I know it is good to be with other believers, but sometimes it doesn't feel worth the pain. I want to know You, but I can't handle most of the Christians I meet. Please give me eyes to see people the way You see them, with love, compassion, forgiveness, and hope. Lead me to a church home just as You are always leading me to my eternal home.*

[Your prayer might be very different from the above, simply let it flow from your heart.]

SESSION EIGHT

HOPE BEYOND
THE PAIN

SESSION EIGHT
HOPE BEYOND THE PAIN

Read Chapter 16:
Hope Beyond the Pain

DISCUSSION QUESTIONS:

1. Have you ever been out of hope? Why?

2. What you think hope looks like in a Christians life?

3. What do you think it means to have hope in Jesus?

4. Do you think people can have hope in difficult circumstances?

5. Has your hope been based on a life without problems?

6. Do you think God's hope is real in this life? Why or why not?

7. Do you believe that the Holy Spirit's presence inside of someone makes a difference in how that person acts and behaves? Can you give an example?

8. To what degree are you aware that God is looking first for a heart that will serve Him and not first for someone who is trying to live a good life?

9. Why is unity in the Christian faith "utterly" necessary?

10. Has God's love ever brought you hope? Describe.

FOR PERSONAL REFLECTION:

1. What parts of your life are being torn apart by disunity—among people or even inside of yourself? How can you bring unity?

2. How can you prepare yourself for the next season of difficulty and pain in your life?

3. Do you feel ready to "move forward at any risk"?

READ:

Father, I desire that they also whom You gave Me may be with Me where I am, that they may behold My glory which You have given Me; for You loved Me before the foundation of the world. O righteous Father! The world has not known You, but I have known You; and these have known that You sent Me. And I have declared to them Your name, and will declare it, that the love with which You loved Me may be in them, and I in them.

(John 17:24–26)

Behold what manner of love the Father has bestowed on us, that we should be called children of God! Therefore the world does not know us, because it did not know Him. Beloved, now we are children of God; and it has not yet been revealed what we shall be, but we know that when He is revealed, we shall be like Him, for we shall see Him as He is. And everyone who has this hope in Him purifies himself, just as He is pure. (1 John 3:1–3)

PONDER:

"Jesus went without comfort so that you might have it. He postponed joy so that you might share in it. He willingly chose isolation so that you might never be alone in your hurt and sorrow. He had no real fellowship so that fellowship might be yours, this moment. This alone is enough cause for great gratitude!"   —Joni Eareckson Tada[20]

"When you have no helpers, see your helpers in God.
When you have many helpers, see God in all your helpers.
When you have nothing but God, see all in God.
When you have everything, see God in everything.
Under all conditions, stay thy heart only on the Lord."
    —Charles H. Spurgeon[21]

"We must accept finite disappointment, but never lose infinite hope."   —Martin Luther King, Jr.

---

20. Joni Eareckson Tada, *A Thankful Heart in a World of Hurt* (Torrance, CA: Rose Publishing, 2012), 10.
21. Charles Spurgeon, *Banner*, Feb. 10, 1978, 8.

AS YOU PRAY:

Does it help to know that God wants to put His hope in you even more than you want it?

> *Father God, I'm overwhelmed with what I see of hope in others. I've never felt that I could ever be like them. All I've ever felt is that You don't like me. But they say that You love everybody, no matter who they are or what they've done. I can't imagine that that is true. They said it's more than possible, but that I can only have it in You, so I'm coming to You to see if I can have what they have.*

[Your prayer might be different from the above, simply let it flow from your heart.]

FURTHER RESOURCES

Bevere, John. *The Bait of Satan*. Lake Mary, FL: Charisma House. 1994.

Bradshaw, John. *Healing the Shame That Binds You*. Deerfield Beach, FL: Health Communications Inc. 1988.

Burchett, Dave. *When Bad Christians Happen to Good People: Where We Have Failed Each Other and How to Reverse the Damage*. Colorado Springs, CO: Multnomah. 2011.

Carr, J. Betty. *You're Loved No Matter What*. San Diego, CA: Black Forest Press. 2000.

Dye, Michael. *The Church: Helping or Hurting?* Genesis. 2015.

Fossum, Merle A. and Marilyn J. Mason. *Facing Shame: Families in Recovery*. New York and London: W. W. Norton & Company. 1986.

Graham, Ruth. *In Every Pew Sits a Broken Heart: Hope for the Hurting*. Nashville, TN: Zondervan. 2008.

Hulsey, Patricia. *Shattering the Shackles of Shame*. Colorado Springs: Harvestime International Network. 2003.

Kluck, Ted, and Ronnie Martin. *The Bridezilla of Christ: What to Do When God's People Hurt God's People.* Colorado Springs, CO: Multnomah. 2016.

Lotz, Anne Graham. *Wounded by God's People: Discovering How God's Love Heals Our Hearts.* Nashville, TN: Zondervan. 2013.

Mansfield, Stephen. *Healing Your Church Hurt: What To Do When You Still Love God But Have Been Wounded by His People.* Carol Stream, IL: Tyndale Momentum. 2012.

McKenzie, John G. *Guilt: Its Meaning and Significance.* Nashville, TN: Abingdon Press. 1962.

Oden, Thomas. *Guilt Free.* Nashville: Abingdon Press. 1980.

Smedes, Lewis B. *Healing the Shame We Don't Deserve.* San Francisco: Harper Collins. 1993.

Tournier, Paul. *Guilt and Grace.* New York: Harper and Row. 1962.

Towns, Elmer L. *What's Right with Church: A Manifesto of Hope.* Grand Rapids, MI: Regal. 2009.

ABOUT THE AUTHORS

Chris Hayward has been the president of Cleansing Stream Ministries (CSM) for over eighteen years. CSM is an organization dedicated to equipping local churches for biblically balanced, sound and effective healing and deliverance ministry. Before his time with CSM, Chris was the founding pastor at Christian Fellowship Church in Mount Vernon, IL, for over twelve years, and has served in pastoral ministry for over thirty-five years. Previous to that, he served as VP Marketing for Word Publishing, and Executive VP of Vision House Publishing. He is also the author of *God's Cleansing Stream* and *The End of Rejection*. He currently makes his home in Santa Clarita, CA, with his wife, Karen. They have three children and four grandchildren.

Ray Beeson is the director of Overcomers Ministries, a teaching ministry with a special emphasis on spiritual warfare and prayer. Ray was a junior high and senior high school mathematics teacher until joining the International Prayer corps with Dick Eastman. When Dick joined World Literature Crusade, Ray went with him, teaching seminars called "The Change the World School of Prayer." In 1983 Ray and four others established Overcomers Ministries, where he remains today. Ray has authored numerous books, including *Signed in His Blood* (Charisma House, 2014), and co-authored *The Hidden Price of Greatness* (Tyndale House, 1991). He lives with his wife, Linda, in Ventura, CA, their home for over thirty-five years. They have four grown children.